FAMOUS FAMILIES™

THE WAYANS BROTHERS

KATHERINE WHITE

 The Rosen Publishing Group, Inc., New York

Published in 2005 by The Rosen Publishing Group, Inc.
29 East 21st Street, New York, NY 10010

First Edition

Library of Congress Cataloging-in-Publication Data

White, Katherine, 1975–
The Wayans brothers / by Katherine White.
    p. cm. — (Famous families)
Includes bibliographical references and index.
ISBN 1-4042-0265-X
1. Wayans, Keenen Ivory. 2. Wayans, Damon. 3. Wayans, Shawn, 1971– 4. Wayans, Marlon. 5 Entertainers—United States—Biography. 6. Motion picture producers and directors—United States—Biography.
I. Title. II. Series.
PN2285.W44 2004
791'.092'273—dc22

                              2004013392

Manufactured in the United States of America

Contents

INTRODUCTION

ALL TOGETHER

In April 1990, FOX television aired the first episode of a new comedy show called *In Living Color*. Airing on Sunday nights at 8 PM, *In Living Color* was comic relief for the whole family—an hour of witty jokes, funny comedy sketches, and colorful dancing. Interestingly, *In Living Color* was also created by a real-life family: the Wayans brothers Keenen, Damon, Shawn, and Marlon as well as their sister Kim directed, produced, wrote, and acted in the show. Since 1990, the four brothers have gone on to direct, produce, and act in dozens of movies and comedy shows—most of the time collaborating on each project.

Today, the Wayans brothers are successful actors, directors, producers, and writers. Yet even though they are part of the glamorous Hollywood scene, they've never lost sight of what's most important. To these four brothers, family and laughter are the ties that bind them to each other. Comedy and humor are lifeblood to the brothers and have been since they were children. The Wayans brothers love comedy, and working with family is both an inspiration as well as the foundation of their success.

FOX's *In Living Color* was a smash hit in the early 1990s. The show pushed the limits of sketch comedy and became an alternative to more mainstream shows such as *Saturday Night Live*. Characters such as Damon Wayans's Homey D. Clown *(left)* left the country laughing for five seasons. The original cast *(inset)* included Damon and Keenen Ivory Wayans, along with their sister Kim.

 **CHAPTER 1**

KEENEN IVORY WAYANS: THE FIRSTBORN

On June 8, 1958, Keenen Ivory Wayans was born in New York City to Howell Wayans, a supermarket manager and Jehovah's Witness, and Elvira Wayans, a homemaker. Little did they know at the time that their firstborn child, in what would become a family of ten children, was going to start a family legacy of comedians, directors, writers, producers, and actors. At the time, the family was living in a small four-bedroom apartment in the Fulton housing projects, in a poor neighborhood on the west side of Manhattan.

Keenen's Early Life

At a very young age, Howell and Elvira knew Keenen was a talented child. His high-energy personality, charisma, and quick wit made him quite charming. Everyone liked being around him. Keenen would entertain and joke around with his nine brothers and

The oldest of ten children, Keenen Ivory Wayans would inspire several of his siblings to try their luck in Hollywood. Keenen's early successes would open doors for each brother and sister who followed.

sisters, keeping them entertained and laughing for hours. But Keenen's personality also had a more rowdy side. "All of us got into trouble for being funny," he recalled in the magazine *Black Collegian*. "We weren't bad kids, but we were always the class clowns . . . and consequently wound up getting chased home a lot for saying the wrong thing to the wrong person."

Keenen might have been a jokester, but he was also a good student. In 1975, he graduated from Sewark Park High School in New York and won a scholarship to the Tuskegee Institute in Alabama, where he majored in engineering. Sometime during his studies in Alabama, Keenen realized his real interests were in the entertainment industry. After a lot of thought, he decided to take the plunge: he left school to pursue his dream of becoming an actor/comedian. At the age of twenty, Keenen Ivory Wayans was off to Hollywood.

Becoming a Comedian

During the late 1970s, young Keenen worked in the entertainment business as a stand-up comic, a career path several of his brothers and sisters would later take as well. While working as a comic, Keenen became friends with Eddie Murphy, a well-known comedian whose star was beginning to rise. Eddie and Keenen quickly formed a deep friendship and began working together on a project that soon skyrocketed both of their careers.

In 1987, Eddie and Keenen teamed up to write and produce a live stand-up performance film called *RAW*. The movie was a major break-through in the world of comedy. Prior to its release, no other comedians had ever released a VHS (video home system) movie of their own performance. At the time, Keenen and Eddie's idea was truly cutting-edge because in 1987, VCRs (video cassette recorders) had only been around for little more than a decade. *RAW* gave Eddie (and Keenen) massive exposure to both audiences and critics around the world.

Even though their idea was original, *RAW* got mixed reactions from the public. It was written for adults and contained foul language. Many of the jokes were considered controversial. Nonetheless, the movie was a hit with reviewers. Critics ranked *RAW* alongside great comedic acts performed by Richard Pryor, one of Keenen's biggest influences. *RAW* became the most profitable comic film ever made.

> ## Fun Facts
>
> When Keenen isn't busy making movies and working in television, he's in the gym. He's an avid weightlifter and he also does yoga three times a week. He is also a vegetarian.

I'm Gonna Git You Sucka

A year later, in 1988, Keenen wrote, produced, and starred in his first solo film project. *I'm Gonna Git You Sucka* was an incredibly popular film about Jack Spade, a young soldier who returns from the army to his old neighborhood. When his younger brother dies, Spade organizes an army and declares war on the neighborhood's most powerful criminal, Mr. Big. The film was released in a wave of similar films like *Do the Right Thing*, which was produced by another young up-and-coming African American named Spike Lee.

Opportunity of a Lifetime

By 1990, Keenen was on his way to the top. His work on *I'm Gonna Git You Sucka* gave him a solid following in Hollywood, and he was considered

I'm Gonna Git You Sucka was a smash hit for Keenen. The hilarious film poked fun at the popular "blaxploitation" films of the 1970s. Keenen even recruited stars from some of those very films that inspired *Sucka*. Pictured here *(left to right)* are Isaac Hayes, Bernie Casey, Keenen, and Jim Brown.

a rising talent both in front of and behind the camera. That same year, FOX Broadcasting approached Keenen and offered him the chance to do whatever he wanted to do. This was an opportunity of a lifetime! In response, Keenen created a groundbreaking sketch comedy show called *In Living Color*. The show also starred his siblings Kim, Damon, Shawn, and Marlon. *In Living Color* would feature other young talent, including Jennifer Lopez, Chris Rock, and Jim Carrey, each of whom would go on to become superstars. The show was a raving success with audiences because it made fun of famous celebrities and also had reoccurring skits of popular characters such as Homey D. Clown and Fire Marshal Bill. But since the show pushed comical boundaries, it was also a target for critics. Many critics complained the show was over-the-top. Chapter 4 will discuss *In Living Color* as well as what it was like for a family to work together on a TV show.

Projects and Family

Keenen left *In Living Color* in 1992 after only two seasons. He had big dreams and leaving the show gave Keenen the time he needed to develop movies. From 1994 to 2001, he starred in, produced, or directed seven films, from *A Low Down Dirty Shame* in 1994 to *Don't Be a Menace to South Central While Drinking Your Juice in the Hood* in 1996. Then, in early 2000 and 2001, came the blockbuster successes of *Scary Movie* and *Scary Movie 2*, both written and directed by Keenen and his brothers Marlon and Shawn.

In Living Color crossed nearly every boundary and made fun of everybody and everything—regardless of color or race. Here, Keenen impersonated former talk-show host Arsenio Hall.

On May 4, 2004, Keenen filed for divorce from Daphne, his wife of three years. The two remain friends and share custody of their four children: Jolie, Keenen Ivory Jr., Nala, and Bella.

Writing a Book and Heading Back to TV

In May 1999, Damon published a book named *Bootleg*, a hilarious compilation about family, children, marriage, and politics. At the time, Damon was married to Lisa Thorner, his wife for more than ten years. With her, Damon had four children: Damon Jr., Michael, Cara, and Kyla. *Bootleg* was a success and quickly landed on the *New York Times* best-seller list.

In 2001, Damon used his family life as an inspiration in his return to television in the hit sitcom *My Wife and Kids*. Damon cocreated, coproduces, and stars in the lead role in the show about the difficulties of trying to raise a traditional family in a not-

Beginning in 2001, Damon started to turn away from movies and concentrate more on his television show, *My Wife and Kids*.

so-traditional world. In 2002, he won the People's Choice Award for Favorite Male Performer in a New Television Series for his role in the show.

17

CHAPTER 3

SHAWN AND MARLON WAYANS: THE YOUNGER BROTHERS

With two older brothers in Hollywood, Shawn and Marlon Wayans were both enticed into careers as comedians. Like Keenen and Damon, the two younger brothers both knew they wanted to act, produce, write, or direct—anything they could do to get the world laughing. These two brothers have teamed up to work together on a variety of projects from TV shows to major films. The younger brothers' careers have also been helped along by their older brothers' inspiration, encouragement, and collaboration in both TV and film.

Shawn Wayans

Shawn Wayans was born on January 19, 1971, in New York City, and is the second-youngest child in the large Wayans family. Like his brothers, Shawn is tall, about 6 feet 2 inches (1.9 meters), and in most

The youngest of the Wayans family, Marlon *(left)* and Shawn have moved out of their brothers' shadows and have become successes in their own right. The brothers' *Scary Movie* films are some of the most successful comedies ever released and have established the brothers' reputation as up-and-coming writers and actors.

photographs, his eyes twinkle with a bit of mischief, showing how much he enjoys laughter and having a good time. Laughter and comedy are family traits.

Choosing Hollywood

By the time Shawn was coming of age in the mid-1980s, his two older brothers Damon and Keenen were already becoming well-known comedians, actors, and filmmakers in Hollywood. The older brothers' success as well as his entire family's deep love for laughter and comedy helped Shawn decide that he, too, wanted to be a comedian and actor. He attended a high school in Manhattan called Bayard Rustin High School for the Humanities, a school known for its excellent acting programs. When Shawn graduated in 1989, he was determined to make a name for himself in Hollywood, too.

A Young Man's Dream Comes to Life

Most actors have a hard time finding a great role that will allow him or her to break into the industry. Going on auditions is tough and tiring work because an actor only has a few minutes to show off his or her talent and leave an excellent impression. Plus, competition is severe. There may be as many as 50 to 100 people trying out for just one role. As a member of a famous family, Shawn had an easier time breaking in to Hollywood. However, no matter what kind of connections his two famous brothers gave him, Shawn would have to prove himself through talent and hard work.

In 1990, Shawn got his first big break when his older brothers came to him and asked him to be part of *In Living Color*. Shawn was more than happy to join the show, especially because he knew his brothers and sister Kim were comic geniuses. This was an incredible opportunity to hone his craft under the guidance of his talented siblings. For three years, Shawn starred as a DJ for the show, spinning records for the show's Fly Girl dancers. His stage name was Sw.1, an old nickname his friends had given to him in high school. Perched above the *In Living Color* set on the DJ platform, looking down on the dancers, Shawn knew comedy was exactly where he belonged. Fortunately, many people agreed.

Shawn's first big break came when he landed a gig as the DJ for his brothers' show *In Living Color*. Here he is in 1990 in a promotional shot with other *In Living Color* regulars Jamie Foxx *(left)* and Steve Park.

Throughout the early 1990s, Shawn landed small parts on other popular TV shows, including *Mac-Gyver*, *Hangin' with Mr. Cooper*, and *Roseanne*. In 1993, after leaving *In Living Color* one season after Damon and Keenen had, Shawn wanted to continue working in television. He turned toward his own family for inspiration and decided to collaborate with his younger brother, Marlon.

Marlon Wayans

Born on July 23, 1972, in New York City, Marlon Wayans is just more than a year younger than Shawn, making him the youngest of the ten

Wayans children. Like the rest of the brothers, Marlon attributes his love for comedy to growing up poor. "The poorer we were, the funnier we were," Marlon said in *State News*. "You had to be funny to get a hug in my house."

Studying Acting

Marlon also knew at a very young age that he loved performing. For high school, he attended one of Manhattan's best drama schools, Fiorello H. La Guardia High School of Music, Art, and Performing Arts. The school is a public high school that prepares students for professional careers in dance, music, or drama. The programs are intensive, and the famous dance movie *Fame* was actually based on the school. Many great actors, including Al Pacino and Liza Minnelli, have graduated from this school.

After graduating from high school, Marlon went off to Howard University in Washington, D.C. There, he enjoyed his studies and was doing well when he entered his sophomore year. However, in 1991, Marlon was bitten by the acting bug, much like his brother before him. He decided to leave school and headed west to work with his brothers on *In Living Color*.

Carving His Own Path

Out of all of the brothers, Marlon's career has benefited the most from his family's collaborations. This mostly has to do with his age. Since he is the youngest child of the family, Damon and Keenen were already working on major film productions and TV shows by the time Marlon arrived in Hollywood. Marlon's next big break after *In Living*

Color came in 1992, when he played a supporting role in *Mo' Money*, a movie Damon wrote, produced, and starred in. In this film, Marlon played Seymour Stewart, the main character's younger brother.

Marlon is aware that many of his first opportunities in Hollywood came from working with his family. At the same time, Marlon works very hard to make sure he still has his own identity in Hollywood. In a 2004 article in *State News*, Marlon told of some of the people who inspire him: "Charlie Chaplin, Richard Pryor and Eddie Murphy were influences. And my brothers, of course. I don't want to emulate anyone else. I have my own flavor and persona. I just want to be Marlon."

Fun Fact: Preparing for a Role

In 1999, before Marlon began work on the drug-addiction film, *Requiem for a Dream*, director Darren Aronofsky asked Marlon to avoid anything that gave him pleasure for thirty days so he could understand the cravings of a drug addict. Marlon gave up everything with sugar in it as well as dating, reading, watching movies and television, and playing video games.

Teaming Up for Television

In 1994, Shawn and Marlon approached Warner Brothers (WB) about doing a TV show. The channel thought the two brothers had a great idea. In January 1995, the first episode of *The Wayans Brothers* aired on the WB. The show chronicled the two brothers' lives as they shared an apartment in New York City. A comedy show based on reality, Marlon and Shawn used their own names and also based their characters loosely on their real-life personalities and relationships.

The show was considered a successful comedy. Even though it never reached number one, it ran for four years.

Into the Movies

Even though Shawn and Marlon were busy with their successful TV show, they still found time to work on other projects. In 1996, they finished writing their first script, called *Don't Be a Menace to South Central While Drinking Your Juice in the Hood.* Once production of the film began, they also executive produced and starred in the feature film.

With the tagline, "Finally, the movie that proves that Justice isn't always Poetic, Jungle Fever isn't always pretty, and Higher Learning can be a waste of time," audiences knew the movie was going to be outrageous. The film is a parody of several other popular African American movies, such as *Boyz N the Hood*, *South Central*, *Menace II Society*, *Higher Learning*, and *Juice*. These movies glamorized life in poor, urban America and dealt with serious issues. With their parody, Marlon and Shawn wanted to tackle the same issues, only lighten the mood a little and do it their way—packed full of comedy. The movie did well at the box office, and both Shawn and Marlon were viewed as up-and-coming comedy filmmakers. However, *Don't Be a Menace* was nothing compared with what the brothers were about to do.

The Dynamic Duo Teams Up Again

In early 2000, Shawn and Marlon teamed up again to write and star in *Scary Movie,* with Keenen directing. In this film, the two brothers parody some of the newest and most popular teen slasher films, including *Scream*, *I Know What You Did Last Summer*, *The Blair*

In spite of the Wayans family's obvious talents, no one expected the runaway success of 2000's *Scary Movie*. The movie parodied favorite teen horror flicks while giving the two youngest Wayans brothers a chance to shine. Here, Shawn and Marlon appear with costar Jon Abrams in a scene from *Scary Movie*.

Witch Project, *The Sixth Sense*, and *The Matrix*. The movie was a smash hit all over the world. In just the opening weekend, the $19 million film grossed $42.5 million, the biggest opening for an R-rated film at the time. Shawn and Marlon had arrived; they were at the top of their comedy world.

CHAPTER 4

COLLABORATION: DOING TV AND FILM TOGETHER

In many ways, the Wayans brothers' comedic legacy began with Keenen. Since he is the oldest child in the family, his decision to become a comedian hugely influenced his younger brothers. In a recent article, on Hollywood.com, Marlon reflects on how Keenen's decision to become a comedian inspired the entire family: "Keenen really crystallized it for us. We watched him on our black-and-white television set, on the Johnny Carson show and we were like, 'Wow! We could be on TV.' And from there, he just helped us turn our dreams into reality."

Keenen has opened a lot of doors for Damon, Marlon, and Shawn. He showed his younger brothers that they could transcend their tough economic background and pursue their dreams. Keenen has also been a never-ending source of support, creativity, and brotherly advice.

Over the years, each of the Wayans brothers has grown into his own and found his own successes in Hollywood. The story of the Wayans family is an inspiring one. The family works together, helping each other out by collaborating, while also exploring and developing individual projects.

But what really launched his brothers' early careers was Keenen's decision to pull from his family's reservoir of talents and have them act and write alongside him in many of his projects. However, even though Keenen served as a foot in the door to Hollywood, Damon, Shawn, and Marlon have all soared on their own. But as their careers took off, each brother has never let go of an important ingredient in their careers as well as their life: working together. Since the mid-1980s, Keenen, Damon, Shawn, and Marlon have continually worked together on successful projects for both the big and small screens.

Confronting Blaxploitation: The First Collaboration

In the mid-1980s, Keenen began writing his first feature film. As he worked, Keenen decided to confront a specific genre of film: blaxploitation. This genre of film uses negative stereotypes to depict African American characters and their lifestyles. Blaxploitation used these negative stereotypes as exploitation to rake in money with films such as *Shaft* and *Superfly*.

In response to blaxploitation, Keenen wanted to show how ridiculous the stereotypes were, so he made a spoof. He wrote, directed, and starred in *I'm Gonna Git You Sucka*. In the movie, he plays Jack Spade, a man who returns from the army to avenge the death of his brother, who died of an overdose of gold chains. The film is meant to be over-the-top, but it was also Keenen's way of confronting the struggle of being a black filmmaker.

In a 1994 interview in the *Black Collegian*, right before the release of *Don't Be a Menace*, Keenen discussed movie critics and race: "Because they don't critique us as filmmakers, everything becomes a social issue. That's not what a filmmaker needs. We don't need you to politicize our work. We need you to give us a fair criticism so we can learn from our mistakes and grow as writers, directors, actors, et cetera. Everything becomes . . . you're speaking for the entire race. I told them I went from being a comedian to the president of the Black race. You're an individual. You don't speak for anybody but yourself, and none of us are trying to speak for our entire race."

I'm Gonna Git You Sucka was also the first project on which Keenen invited a family member to work. In *Sucka*, younger brother Damon plays Leonard, a friend of Keenen's character. Keenen and Damon worked incredibly well together. Only a few years later, the two would find themselves working together in a spectacular TV show.

In Living Color: Breaking Boundaries

In 1990, when FOX gave Keenen the opportunity to do anything he wanted, Keenen knew he wanted to do something different—something really different. Keenen wanted to do a show that pushed boundaries but also made people laugh. Inspired by television shows such as *Laugh In*, *The Carol Burnett Show*, and *Saturday Night Live*, Keenen's brainstorming soon led to the creation of *In Living Color*, a sketch comedy show. When it was time to pick the cast, Keenen remembered his great working relationship with Damon on *I'm Gonna Git You Sucka*. Keenen soon realized his family was basically a pool of talented writers and performers.

A Cast Made Up of Family

Keenen invited his entire family to work with him on *In Living Color*. Keenen was billed as the creator of the show, and he and Damon were

The Wayans' formula for success is a delicate mixture of wackiness and social satire. Here, on *In Living Color*, Damon hams it up with costar David Allen Grier.

two of the show's talented writers. Kim, Shawn, and Marlon acted in most of the skits as did Keenen and Damon. As soon as the show hit the airwaves in April 1990, it was a huge success. At the same time, *In Living Color* attracted controversy because it confronted black stereotypes by making fun of them. Some of the more memorable sketches included "The Do-It-Yourself Milli Vanilli Kit" and "The Michael Jackson Potato Head Kit." Suffice it to say, *In Living Color* made fun of celebrities.

Working Together

One would think that working on a TV show with your own family would be stressful and at times extremely difficult. But the cast of *In Living Color* was just like the loving family the Wayans brothers grew up in. "We're pretty tight," explained Keenen in an interview in the *Black Collegian*. "That's all we had. We grew up in an impoverished background and didn't have a lot of toys or a lot of anything other than good laughs. And the thing that I think helped us to get beyond our environment was that we were able to have closeness and the support system within the house. Everybody constantly looking out for one another." That support system translated to the set of *In Living Color.*

Awards and Reverberations

In 1990, Hollywood acknowledged Keenen's talent when he won an Emmy Award in the category of Outstanding Variety, Music, or Comedy Program for *In Living Color*. Hosted by the Academy of Television Arts and Sciences, an Emmy is one of the most prestigious awards in television. The next year, he won a NOVA Award for the category of Most Promising Producer in Television. Given by the Liberty Livewire NOVA Award group, the award is given to a producer who has made an early career breakthrough or has made a stunning debut into the industry. In 1992, Keenen and his brother Damon ended up leaving the show because of creative differences with their producers. The show continued for two more years without them. After Keenen and Damon left, *In Living Color* never recovered its initial popularity and was eventually canceled in 1994.

The Wayans Brothers

In 1995, Shawn and Marlon followed in the steps of their oldest brother and created their own TV show, *The Wayans Brothers*. The show was loosely based on their own lives growing up in an animated, tight-knit family. Starring as themselves, Shawn and Marlon share a one-bedroom brownstone in New York City and have a hard time agreeing on anything. At age twenty-four, Shawn's character is the organized and independent one because he owns his own news-stand. He has big dreams of becoming a successful businessman and is looking for true love. Marlon's character is the exact opposite: he takes life as it comes, living moment to moment, and rarely has more than two pennies to rub together. With the two brothers living at opposite ends of the spectrum, the show concentrates on how

often the two brothers disagree. A lot of comedy comes out of their disagreements.

In reality, Shawn and Marlon work together exceptionally well. They are supportive and open when writing and acting together. In a recent *State News* article, Shawn shared one of the keys to their success, "We are all very supportive of each other—we aren't in competition. We don't try to say, 'I'm funnier than you.' Family is key. If you have love for your family, then you'll have love for others." *The Wayans Brothers* had a successful four-year run until it went off the air in 1999.

Scary Movie

In the late 1990s, Shawn, Marlon, and Keenen teamed up again. With Shawn and Marlon as the writers and Keenen as the director, *Scary Movie* became another phenomenal collaboration for the Wayans family. While doing research for the film, Marlon, Shawn, and Keenen watched more than 160 classic (and not-so-classic) horror films. At first, their research was a ton of fun—they were getting paid to watch horror films! But after viewing a 100 films, the excitement wore off and watching the horror films felt like work. However, their work paid off. In 2000, when *Scary Movie* was released, it grossed $153 million in the United States and $100 million in Europe. Audiences loved the film. The movie only cost $19 million to make, so it made an enormous amount of money. Even though *Scary Movie 2* was a sequel, which tends not to do as well, it brought in a solid $125 million. Then in 2003, audiences went wild for *Scary Movie 3*. The first weekend brought in $49 million.

Working Together: Handling Conflicts

Working with anyone can be a challenge, but writing, acting, and producing a show with your own family can be an even bigger one. During these challenging times, Shawn says that he and Marlon try to talk through their conflicts. In an E!Online article, Shawn shared in his usual lighthearted way: "It could be tense for a minute, then he goes off, sits with his thing and I sit with what he just told me and then we come back and have a little friendly summit. Like, 'I hear what you're saying, but here's what I'm trying to say to you.' And then he'll digest what I'm saying, and we hug and kiss." This is just one example of how the Wayans brothers work together. They respect one another's opinions and always remember that humor is a great way to break the tension.

Overall, the Wayans family works together as a team. They are supportive and open with one another, and they work hard to respect and appreciate one another's talents. They each have strengths and weaknesses and they try to cultivate each other's greatest strengths when they work together. In an E!Online article, Shawn shares what makes each brother stand out: "Well, with Damon, when it comes to stand-up, that's his world. Keenen, when it comes to putting things together, structuring jokes, nobody is better. When it comes to coming up with ideas, nobody is better than Shawn. He is brilliant, most of the movies we've done have been Shawn's ideas. I'm good at coming up with wacky characters and funny dialogue."

CHAPTER 5

CURRENT PROJECTS AND WHAT'S UP NEXT

The past few years have been incredibly busy for the Wayans brothers. As usual, they've been working hard to push new boundaries as comedic performers and directors, both in television and film. They have also continued to work together, inspiring one another to push the limits of creativity and comedy. In fact, almost all of the projects they are currently working on are collaborations within the family. So, what have they worked on most recently and what might they do in the future?

My Wife and Kids

How does Damon Wayans keep busy these days? Damon fills his days as the cocreator, star, and executive producer of the highest-rated African American TV show currently on the air, *My Wife and Kids*. The show debuted in 2001, and has been running strong

After four successful seasons on ABC, Damon is showing no signs of slowing down while starring in his own sitcom, *My Wife and Kids*. The hit show mixes good old Wayans humor, family values, and an excellent cast, such as Tisha Campbell-Martin, who costars as Damon's wife, Jay.

The Sister in Show-biz: Kim Wayans

Kim Wayans was born in 1961, in New York City. Like her brothers, she knew that Hollywood was where she belonged. She got her start in television doing cameos on *China Beach*, a TV show about a group of army nurses working during the Vietnam War.

Soon, Kim was a regular on shows such as *In the House* as well as *A Different World*. Currently, she is a writer, director, and story editor for Damon's show *My Wife and Kids*.

since. In fact, the show is considered the anchor show for the Wednesday night sitcom lineup for ABC. *My Wife and Kids*, which Damon admits was loosely based on the trials and errors of his own marriage and family life, is about a father and professional, Michael Kyle, played by Damon, Jay Kyle (Tisha Campbell-Martin), and their three children.

The show deals with very real and sometimes controversial issues, like religion and teenage pregnancy. In a recent episode, the Kyles find out their eighteen-year-old son, Junior, and his girlfriend are expecting a baby. The Kyles are initially devastated and disappointed but soon realize that teenage pregnancy is an issue that millions of families face. In the same episode, their oldest daughter, Claire, is struggling with her judgmental and headstrong religious boyfriend who is critical of her brother and his girlfriend for "sinning" by having premarital sex.

Because *My Wife and Kids* deals with some very sensitive issues, it sometimes draws a lot of criticism. In the face of this criticism, the production team has made it clear it is dedicated to putting out a show to which everyone can relate. When asked to describe the Kyles, Damon reflected in *Ebony* magazine, "We're not the perfect family, we're just trying to work out problems that appeal to people. It's universal—and that's the great thing about it." The show is not only popular in the United States but has captured a huge audience in the United Kingdom and Europe as well.

As the popularity of *My Wife and Kids* grows, so, too, does the list of Damon Wayans's successful projects. Some might say that with his most recent successes Damon is on top of the film and TV world, but Damon feels otherwise. He feels the path to success comes with a price tag he is not yet ready to pay. When asked about his successes, he shares in *Ebony* magazine, "I don't ever want to be number one because once you become number one, you start to change. You get scrutinized on every-thing you do, and you're suddenly afraid to take chances. I need to take chances. I need to work. I don't want to be a superstar."

Marlon is beginning to establish himself as a diverse and accomplished actor. His roles have varied from playing a drug addict in *Requiem for a Dream* to a bungling thief in *The Ladykillers*. He is shown above with J. K. Simmons.

The Ladykillers

In March 2004, Marlon starred in *The Ladykillers*, a Coen brothers production. Joel and Ethan Coen are famous for directing quirky and

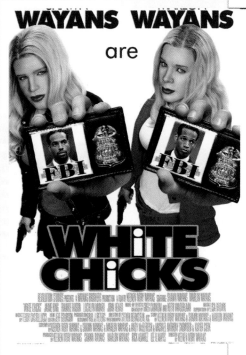

In 2004, Marlon and Shawn teamed up again for another wacky comedy in *White Chicks*. Although slammed by critics, the film nonetheless drew large audiences.

oddball films including *Fargo*, *O Brother, Where Art Thou?*, and *Raising Arizona*. *The Ladykillers* is a remake of the 1955 British movie comedy about a group of underachievers turned con artists planning a massive heist of a New Orleans riverboat.

Working with the Coen brothers gave Marlon the opportunity to work in a completely different environment from his past works, which were mostly with his family. In a recent article on MTV.com, Marlon was asked to compare the different directorial styles of his brother Keenen with the Coen brothers': "Keenen does jigsaw puzzles, and the Coens do crossword puzzles. The Coens know all the answers before they even start, very organized and laid out. We kinda figure it out as we go. We know what we want but we have fun and play around with it more."

White Chicks

Despite work on separate projects, Shawn and Marlon have managed to squeeze in enough time to star in Keenen's latest writing and directorial creation, *White Chicks*, which was released the summer of 2004. In this film, Shawn and Marlon play New York City FBI (Federal Bureau of Investigation) agents and brothers who foul up a major drug bust. As punishment, the brothers are reassigned to work as escorts for two wealthy sisters Brittany and Tiffany Wilson (a spoof on the famous Hilton sisters, Paris and Nicky).

Their True Inspiration

The Wayans family is unique. On one hand, it is unique because it has some of the most talented comedians and filmmakers in Hollywood. But, it is also exceptional because its members know their roots and they genuinely appreciate their family ties. When talking about their parents, Damon shares how inspirational both mother and father were to their sons. In *Black Collegian*, Damon explained that inspiration runs deep: "My mother is a woman who was always encouraging and always made you feel good about anything you did and made you feel like you could do anything."

Damon also explains how his father gave his sons motivation: "And my father was a guy who was a dreamer and never gave up on his dreams. He always wanted to have his own business, and we would watch him start and fail time and time again. But he never stopped trying. And he always would say things to us that were very profound, things that would stick in our heads. Things like, 'if you fall just get up and dust yourself off and go for it again.' When you see an example of that before you, when you see somebody get up every day and do it, then it further reinforces what they've been telling you." Living by those words, the Wayans brothers have far surpassed their dreams.

1958	• June 8, Keenen Ivory Wayans is born in New York City.
1960	• September 4, Damon Wayans is born in New York City.
1971	• January 19, Shawn Wayans is born in New York City.
1972	• July 23, Marlon Wayans is born in New York City.
1984	• Damon lands his first film role as a street vendor selling bananas in *Beverly Hills Cop*.
1987	• Eddie Murphy and Keenen team up to write and produce the comic film *RAW*.
1988	• Keenen writes, produces, and stars in his first solo film project, *I'm Gonna Git You Sucka*; he invites Damon to act in the film as well.
1990	• Keenen creates a groundbreaking sketch comedy show, *In Living Color*; five of the Wayans family work on the TV show; Damon wins an Emmy for his work on *In Living Color*.
1992	• Damon writes, produces, and stars in the comedy *Mo' Money*.
1995	• Shawn and Marlon create the hit show *The Wayans Brothers*.
1996	• Shawn and Marlon write the hit *Don't Be a Menace to South Central While Drinking Your Juice in the Hood*.
1999	• Damon writes a book titled *Bootleg*; it eventually hits the *New York Times* best-seller list.
2000	• Shawn and Marlon team up to write and star in *Scary Movie*; Keenen directs.
2001	• Damon creates the hit ABC sitcom *My Wife and Kids*.
2004	• Marlon stars in the movie *The Ladykillers*.
	• Keenen writes and directs Shawn and Marlon in *White Chicks*.

FILMOGRAPHY

Keenen Ivory Wayans

2004	• White Chicks
2001	• Scary Movie 2
2000	• Scary Movie
1997	• Most Wanted
1996	• Don't Be a Menace to South Central While Drinking Your Juice in the Hood and The Glimmer Man
1994	• A Low Down Dirty Shame
1991	• The Five Heartbeats
1988	• I'm Gonna Git You Sucka
1987	• Hollywood Shuffle and RAW

Notable Television

1990–1992	• In Living Color
1997	• The Keenen Ivory Wayans Show
1983	• For Love and Honor

Damon Wayans

2003	• Marci X
2000	• Bamboozled
1999	• Goosed and Harlem Aria
1996	• Bulletproof, The Great White Hype, Celtic Pride, and Don't Be a Menace to South Central While Drinking Your Juice in the Hood
1995	• Major Payne
1994	• Blankman
1993	• Last Action Hero
1992	• Mo' Money
1991	• The Last Boy Scout
1990	• Look Who's Talking Too
1989	• Earth Girls Are Easy
1988	• Colors, I'm Gonna Git You Sucka, and Punchline
1987	• Roxanne and Hollywood Shuffle
1984	• Beverly Hills Cop

FILMOGRAPHY

Notable Television

2001	• *My Wife and Kids*
1990	• *In Living Color*
1989	• *One Night Stand*
1985	• *Saturday Night Live*

Shawn Wayans

2004	• *White Chicks*
2001	• *Scary Movie 2*
2000	• *Scary Movie*
1999	• *New Blood*
1996	• *Don't Be a Menace to South Central While Drinking Your Juice in the Hood*
1988	• *I'm Gonna Git You Sucka*

Notable Television

1995	• *The Wayans Brothers*
1990	• *In Living Color*

Marlon Wayans

2004	• *White Chicks* and *The Ladykillers*
2001	• *Scary Movie 2*
2000	• *Scary Movie, Dungeons & Dragons*, and *Requiem for a Dream*
1998	• *Senseless*
1997	• *The Sixth Man*
1996	• *Don't Be a Menace to South Central While Drinking Your Juice in the Hood*
1994	• *Above the Rim*
1992	• *Mo' Money*
1988	• *I'm Gonna Git You Sucka*

Notable Television

1995	• *The Wayans Brothers*
1990	• *In Living Color*

GLOSSARY

blaxploitation A combination of "black" and "exploitation"; coined in the 1970s when a series of films were produced that depicted African American characters and their lifestyles with negative stereotypes.

cameo A small theatrical role usually performed by a well-known actor and often limited to a single scene.

charisma A special magnetic charm or appeal.

collaborate To work jointly with others.

genre A category of artistic, musical, or literary composition characterized by a particular style, form, or content.

Jehovah's Witness A religion that believes in the return of Christ and actively practices evangelism.

legacy Something transmitted by or received from an ancestor or predecessor.

parody A type of art or medium in which the style of an author or work imitates other work or situations for comic effect or ridicule.

satire Humor used to expose and exaggerate shortcomings in a subject.

sitcom Radio or TV comedy series that involves a continuing cast of characters in a succession of episodes.

skit A short satirical or humorous story acted out.

spoof A light, humorous parody.

stereotype A standardized mental picture that is held in common by members of a group and that represents an oversimplified opinion, prejudiced attitude, or critical judgment.

Web sites

Due to the changing nature of Internet links, the Rosen Publishing Group, Inc., has developed an online list of Web sites related to the subject of this book. This site is updated regularly. Please use this link to access the list:

http://www.rosenlinks.com/fafa/wabr

Diawara, Martha, ed. *Black American Cinema*. New York: Routledge, 1993.

Johnson, Manthia. *Careers in the Movies*. New York: The Rosen Publishing Group, 2001.

Karnick, Kristine Brunovska, and Henry Jenkins, eds. *Classical Hollywood Comedy*. New York: Routledge, 1994.

Nagle, Jeanne. *Careers in Television*. New York: The Rosen Publishing Group, 2001.

Wayans, Damon, and David Asbery. *Bootleg*. New York: HarperCollins, 2000.

Wayans, Keenen I. and Nelson George. *In Living Color: The Authorized Companion to the Fox TV Series*. New York: Warner Books, 1991.

Wayans, Shawn, Chris Spencer and Suli McCullough. *150 Ways to Tell If You're Ghetto*. Boston: DTP, 1997.

BIBLIOGRAPHY

Blackfilm.com. "The LadyKillers." 2004. Retrieved January 30, 2004 (http://www.blackfilm.com/20040326/reviews/theladykillers.shtml).

Bowen, Kit. "The Wayans Way." January 2004. Retrieved January 26, 2004 (http://www.hollywood.com/celebs/story/t4/feature/1746987).

Collier, Aldore. *Ebony*. "My Wife and Kids Backstage at No. 1 Black TV Show." December 2003. Retrieved January 28, 2004 (http://www.findarticles.com/cf_0/m1077/2_59/110962920/p1/article.jhtml).

IMDB. "Biography of Damon Wayans." 2004. Retrieved January 26, 2004 (http://www.imdb.com/name/nm0001834/).

IMDB. "Biography for Keenen Ivory Wayans." 2004. Retrieved January 27, 2004 (http://www.imdb.com/name/nm0005540/bio).

IMDB. "Don't Be a Menace to South Central While Drinking Your Juice in the Hood." 2004. Retrieved January 26, 2004 (http://www.imdb.com/title/tt0116126/).

Rotten Tomatoes. "Eddie Murphy RAW." 1998. Retrieved January 13, 2004 (http://ofcs.rottentomatoes.com/click/movie1006467/reviews.php?critic = movies&sortby = default&page = 1&rid = 254205).

 **INDEX**

About the Author

Katherine White is a freelance writer and editor in and around New York City. She lives in Jersey City, New Jersey.

Photo Credits

Cover (top and bottom), pp. 4, 6, 10, 11, 12, 15, 17, 18, 21, 25, 26, 30, 34, 37, 38 © Everett Collection, Inc.; p. 1 (background) © Royalty-Free/Corbis; p. 1 © AP World Wide Photos; p. 16 © Bureau L.A. Collection/Corbis.

Designer: Nelson Sá; **Editor:** Charles Hofer;
Photo Researcher: Nelson Sá

B White, Katherine
WAY The Wayans Brothers

DATE DUE BC 19483